Sylvia Shap

Some Members of My Family

May 31 – July 10, 1988

Marie de Alcuaz, Curator
Essay by Jim Edwards

Los Angeles Municipal Art Gallery

An exhibition organized by the Los Angeles Municipal Art Gallery, City of Los Angeles Cultural Affairs Department.
This catalogue was sponsored by a donation from Eileen and Peter Norton.

Table of Contents

Works Illustrated

Cover Illustration:
Summer Self, 1979
Oil on panel, 36 x 49¼

Sylvia Shap: Some Members of My Family
Los Angeles Municipal Art Gallery
May 31 – July 10, 1988

Catalogue Design: Jerry McMillan, Pasadena, CA
Photography: Tomás O'Brien, Los Angeles, CA
Typographer: Type Works, Inc. Pasadena, CA
Color Separations: International Art Services, Inc.
   Woodland Hills, CA
Lithographer: Typecraft, Inc., Pasadena, CA
Paper: Quintessence Dull Book and Cover
Type: Cheltenham family
Catalogues Printed: 1000

Library of Congress Number 88-050413
ISBN 0-936429-10-0

Lady on Opening Night, 1980. Pastel and oil on panel, 59 x 42, Collection of the Victoria Regional Museum, Texas (not included in exhibition)

Preface and Acknowledgments

It is with great pleasure that the Los Angeles Municipal Art Gallery presents *Sylvia Shap: Some Members of My Family*. I have admired Sylvia's work for many years, watching it evolve and hoping that, when the moment was right, we would be able to produce a major exhibition of her work. I am delighted that this moment has arrived.

The Los Angeles Municipal Art Gallery is dedicated to organizing exhibitions illustrating the significant developments and achievements of living Southern California artists. Sylvia Shap is one of our finest artists. Her mastery of contemporary portraiture demonstrates an astute combination of seer and painter. She is able to capture the inner spirit of her subjects, unveiling general truths through the look in their eyes or the gesture of their hands. We are very grateful to the artist and all the "members of her family" for allowing us to bring them together to give tribute to the work of Sylvia Shap.

Of primary importance to an exhibition is the documentation of this ephemeral moment. Peter and Eileen Norton were responsible for making this a reality. On behalf of the Los Angeles Municipal Art Gallery Associates and the Cultural Affairs Department of the City of Los Angeles I wish to express my warmest thanks to the Nortons for their generous contribution to this catalogue.

Our thanks are also extended to Jim Edwards for his eloquent essay and to Jerry McMillan for the design and consultation of this catalogue. At the Municipal Art Gallery, I would like to especially thank Carla Fantozzi, Scott Canty, Patricia Kay Adams, Steve Clugston and Sidney Taylor for their magnanimous efforts. Special thanks are also due Rodney Punt, our General Manager and Judy Weinstein, President of the Associates for their guidance and support of this project.

Marie de Alcuaz
Curator
Los Angeles Municipal Art Gallery

Artist's Acknowledgement

I want to express my most heartfelt gratitude to all of you who have given me encouragement and support: my immediate family, friends, kind acquaintances and varied professionals. Very special thanks to Marie de Alcuaz, Eileen and Peter Norton and all who worked to make this exhibition and catalogue possible. I must also thank all of my patrons and subjects for their appreciation, cooperation and trust; each one of you have taught me so much and helped me with my own personal perspectives. I feel like you are all members of my family.

Sylvia Shap

Lenders

Linda and Gary Briskman
Judy and Edouard Brush
Franc Caggiano
Ariel Kelsey Dill
Joan and Jerry Doren
David and Wena Dows
Lorrie and Richard Gurewitz
Selma Holo
Douglas and Sandi Jackson
David G. Johns "Buck"
Nancy and Bernie Kattler
Arnold William Klein, M.D.
Dan Logan
Patricia J. Maslon
Jim Moore
John Moshay, Jr.
Eileen and Peter Norton
Nanci and Kenneth Powell
Joan and Jack Quinn Collection
Sylvia Shap
Mr. and Mrs. Samuel A. Storm
Jim Ward
Marcia S. Weisman Collection
Mr. and Mrs. Billy Wilder

California Male, 1983. Oil on canvas, 74 x 50

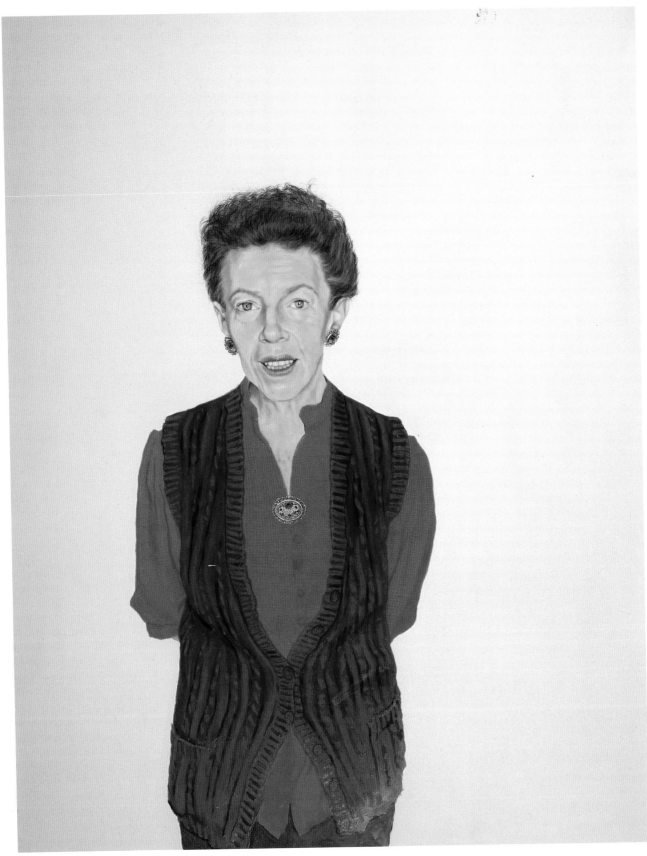

My Mother, 1987. Oil on panel, 48½ x 38½

The Jackson Kids, 1986. Oil on panel, 81 x 68

Madame X, 1987. Oil on panel, 96 x 48 (not included in exhibition)

Likeness and Beyond: The Art of
SYLVIA SHAP

The art of portraiture in its truest sense begins with an act of collaboration with the subject facing the camera or easel and the artist attempting to solicit a truthfulness about the person portrayed. The commissioned portrait is especially challenging for an artist since one would assume that giving satisfaction to likeness and vanity is an understood prerequisite. Beyond mere recognition, portraiture is really about a way of seeing. Since sight is the busiest of our senses, freezing a human image in a photograph or painting constitutes for the artist a grievous responsibility of melding the topical and temporal with truthfulness. The process of this required scrutiny calls for a kind of exactitude to which we are not normally subject. Neither artist nor sitter wants to avoid visual fact and yet ultimately the artist's attempt to fuse outer and inner realities will hopefully produce an image of the sitter that goes beyond likeness.

One of the great burdens facing the contemporary portrait artist is that advanced technologies have encouraged us to glance rather than to look. The plethora of faces and figures which infuse our daily lives through movies, television and all forms of advertising do not encourage the attentiveness associated with traditional forms of portraiture. The real advantage of portrait photography and painting is that it affords the artist an opportunity to stop our eye, to take an isolated moment in time and give it a sense of monumentality.

Los Angeles artist Sylvia Shap has claimed as her domain the art of portraiture. Her life-sized portraits of contemporary men, women and children are precisely rendered and confrontational in the sense that her subjects always look out directly towards the viewer. We notice immediately that the model is cognizant of their presence in Shap's compositions. There is no turning away or gazing off into the distance. We meet her subjects eye to eye, an invitation for the viewer to physically and psychologically "size up" the artist's subjects in the process of looking at the paintings. We also notice that Shap always places her figures against blank evenly colored backgrounds, a device she shares with the photographer Richard Avedon and which helps bring full attention to her models' demeanor, to their stance, gesture and attitude. She also shares with Avedon a meticulous attention to surface detail, although Shap's figures collectively seem much more optimistic than Avedon's characters which more often appear morose and somehow psychologically wounded. Both artists brilliantly render the visible. The fidelity of surface detail is so articulated that it forms an aesthetic in itself. Avedon acknowledges the importance of surface when he states, "my photographs don't go below the surface. They

2 Sisters, 1987. Drawing on painted background, 48¼ x 70⅛

don't go below anything. They're readings of what's on the surface. I have good faith in surfaces, a good one is full of clues."[1] Faith in surfaces notwithstanding, Sylvia Shap would add to Avedon's statement the recognition that the interior also informs the exterior; she has said, "I feel the two realms of outward appearance and the inner self are interchangeable."[2]

Shap trained her visual memory by working from life until 1973. But, now Shap begins her creative process with the camera which she uses as a sketch or a drawing to jog her recall of the subject. The heart of the painting emerges from the artist's memory of the subject. She asks her subjects to choose their own attire and their favorite color, which is used in her compositions as the background color. The posing is casual and straight on. She establishes a collaboration by her interactions with the subjects. When it comes to the paintings and drawings themselves, she uses different media within the same composition, exploiting the colors and textures of oil, watercolor, gouache, pastel, ink and colored pencil. Background color becomes her source of light as well as a key to the subject's mood.

At first glance we may react to Sylvia Shap's paintings with a sense of easy recognition. They conform to what Edwin Denby referred to as "the optic flash associated with advertising."[3] In this sense, Shap's work can be related to Pop Art's ability to be immediately recognizable. But Shap's paintings also always remain personal in that first and foremost they are portraits of specific people. Her clients have commissioned her to produce a likeness but their ease of gesture may conform as much to our ideals of success and self esteem as they do to the model's own bearing.

Shap's paintings allude to the "cult of the now". Many of her models are fashion conscious and express a contemporaneity which Alex Katz also recognizes in his work. Irving Sandler has also acknowledged that when the private becomes public, social status is at stake. Sandler has written, "in an essay which consummately defined dandyism as a cultural phenomenon, Baudelaire wrote that the essential attribute of the dandy is to be a sharp observer of contemporary society and culture, particularly attentive to what makes it contemporary."[4] Shap's paintings, *Gary Briskman* and *California Male* conform to our sense of dandyism — our image of the California man as suntanned, virile and continually with it. Such generalizations can inspire satire, but in her portraits of both men and women Shap, like Alex Katz, often has subjects who collectively form the subculture of her own environment. Sylvia Shap is also careful not to let the sitter's own ego completely dominate. She skillfully composes each painting to maximize or minimize the background space allotted her subject. As a portrait artist her craft has not drifted into formula. Each painting varies in size. Using a compositional device favored by Degas a hundred years ago, Shap is not afraid to crop her models at the picture's edge. By eliminating all objects from the background of her paintings except the figure itself, Shap accentuates the model's sense of gesture. In the painting *Dan Logan*, we are aware that Mr. Logan is sitting on a couch, and yet by eliminating the piece of furniture itself, Shap has emphasized the gesture of his outstretched arms and the contour of his act of sitting which greatly heightens the very "couchiness" of the pose.

Sylvia Shap has also examined human comedy. In her painting *Kenny and Nanci*, the models are frozen as in a photographic snapshot. Nanci is pulling on a chain wrapped around Kenny's neck, but the sensation is one of having interrupted two people at horseplay. They are looking directly towards us, each grinning ear to ear. As she cinches the chain around Kenny's neck, Nanci quite sensuously leans back towards him. The act of bondage is playfully symbolic, and also quite possibly the root of some private joke. In all of Shap's group portraits of husbands and wives, friends and relatives, the artist creates a sense of closeness — a reassuring arm on a shoulder or some gesture of caring.

At times, Shap's subjects will pose in a theatrical garb. In *Sam as Napoleon,* we see a full figure pose, the model with his legs parted, straight-backed, cockily looking out towards us. This portrait seems to invite the viewer to challenge the model. By his determined bearing and defiant gaze, Sam's pose is a close resemblance to Franz Hals' masterful portrait *Claes Duyst Van Voorhout.*[5] But unlike the 17th century brewery master whose abundant ego Hals has compositionally allowed to completely fill the canvas, in *Sam as Napoleon*, Shap has cut her subject down to size by placing him in the lower right-hand corner. The expansive warm white field behind Sam can be imagined as nothing more than a studio prop. Sam may fit into Napoleon's clothes and strike an appropriate pose, but he is acting, or is he?

There is a certain hygienic quality which surrounds Shap's subjects, a result of her love of clear light, strong color and the youthful vigor of life in Southern California. In her painting *Ariel Dill*, little Ariel in a purple blouse and sweat pants stretches her hands over her head in a natural child-like gesture, a gesture which Roy Lichtenstein took advantage of in his classic 1961 pop painting *Girl with Ball.*[6] Lichtenstein's image was actually derived from a *New York Times* advertisement for a health and honeymoon resort in Mt. Pocono, Pennsylvania.[7] Shap's portrait of Ariel on the other hand is a personal, rather than a public tribute. In her painting the *Jackson Kids,* Shap has captured the three ages of youth, including her subjects' progressive states of quizzical wonder, quiet reserve, and nearly aloof self-assurance.

Certainly one of the strongest portraits in this exhibition is *My Mother.* Here Sylvia Shap has infused the painting's surface with sympathy. In her rendering of her mother, Shap has dispensed with all generalized notions and the niceness that one expects of a portrait. In *My Mother,* we observe a mature woman, her body in ¾ view facing us directly with her hands folded behind her back. She looks toward us with a vulnerable but knowing gaze. There is a keen sense of introspection in Shap's rendering of her mother's features, meticulous in its denseness and complexity. This is the kind of attentiveness to perception which a gifted artist can at times solicit from a portrait. So rich and specific in detail that it invites inspection and speculation, *My Mother,* is a memorable portrait and certainly the result of love and understanding between mother and daughter. This personal relationship allows the sitter to submit herself to the artist with unquestioned trust allowing the artist to dispense with any form of artifice.

The paintings that comprise this exhibition trace the course of Sylvia Shap's development as a portrait artist over the last ten years. Her fidelity to objective truth carries with it a wide range of emotions. Collectively this body of work represents a cultural statement. Sylvia Shap has reached beyond the particulars of a photorealistic technique and her subjects affect us in human terms: she has stated herself, "I consider myself to be a documentary artist more than a portraitist. My conceptual overview in painting goes beyond the purpose of supplying the subject with a likeness. Although likeness is certainly important, I see each image as part of a continuum of statements about our culture and life in general."[8] What makes Shap's task so particularly difficult is that we as her audience bring with us a demand for exactitude and a certain dread that such graphic precision will reveal truths we would just as well ignore.

Finally, Sylvia Shap offers us her own likeness. In the painting of 1979, *Summer Self,* she presents herself in ¾ view wearing a gaily flowered blouse opened to reveal a yellow brief and a string of sea shells hanging from her neck. An orange tiger lily is placed just behind her ear, a colorful complement to her dark hair and the field of coral red which surrounds her. Sylvia's features bear a striking resemblance to Goya's portrait of *Dona Narcisa Baranana de Giocoecha.*[9] Both exhibit gracefully rounded faces with beautiful dark eyes and the same delineation of eyebrows and nose. The difference can be seen in the mouth and pose. Goya's youthful relative is decked out in her finest. Upright and noble in stature, she has given herself over completely to her famous artist and her own acknowledged beauty. Sylvia in contrast expresses a more quizzical look and her closed lips are set with a certain pinch of diminution. *Summer Self,* is a self appraisal which acknowledges the fact that this is an artist who even in those moments of leisure and dress up must be constantly aware that she has chosen as her profession the cliche-ridden field of portraiture. Her expression is that of a seer, an artist aware of the grand tradition of portrait painting.

Sylvia Shap is one of our country's best portrait painters, capable of rendering all types of likeness, who through the investigation of the particular and the self has offered us a legacy dedicated to contemporary life.

Jim Edwards

Brown Curator of Contemporary Art
San Antonio Museum of Art
San Antonio, Texas

April, 1988

Notes

1. Jim Edwards, *About Face,* catalogue for the exhibit *About Face,* Art Museum of South Texas, Corpus Christi, Texas, 1984 N.P.

2. Peter Clothier, *Looking at Others,* Artweek, Volume 10, Number 19, Oakland, California, May 12, 1979, P. 3.

3. Edwin Denby, *Katz: Collage, Cut out, Cut up,* Art News, New York, January 1965, P. 44.

4. Irving Sandler, *Alex Katz,* Harry N. Abrams, Inc., New York, 1979, P. 45.

5. The Painting *Claes Duyst Van Voorhout,* c. 1638 by Franz Hals, oil on canvas, 31¾ x 26, The Metropolitan Museum of Art, New York City.

6. The painting *Girl with Ball,* 1961 by Roy Lichtenstein, oil on canvas, 60½ x 36½, Collection of Philip Johnson, New York City.

7. Lucy Lippard, *Pop Art,* Frederick A. Praeger, New York, 1966, P. 80.

8. Jim Edwards, *About Face,* catalogue for the exhibit *About Face,* Art Museum of South Texas, Corpus Christi, Texas, 1984, N.P.

9. The painting *Dona Narcisa Baranana de Giocoecha,* 1796 by Francisco Goya, oil on canvas, 113 x 78 cm, Metropolitan Museum of Art, New York.

A Woman at Narita, 1987. Oil on panel, 44⁹/₁₆ x 47⅝

Kenny and Nanci, 1983. Oil on panel, 47⅝ x 45½

Corky and Bill, 1979. Oil on panel, 48 x 54 (not included in exhibition)

The Nortons, 1987. Oil pastel and drawing on painted background, 45 x 77

The Dorens, 1987. Drawing with painted background, 40 x 89

Pat Maslon, 1985. Drawing with painted background, 35½ x 52½

The Wilders, 1982. Oil on panel, 42½ x 70

David Johns, 1980. Pastel with painted background, 39 x 26

Catalogue of the Exhibition

Dimensions are noted in inches,
height precedes width.

Dan Logan, 1977
Oil on panel, 36 x 72
Courtesy of Jim Moore

Jim, 1978
Oil on panel, 40⅛ x 35¾
Courtesy of Jim Ward

Summer Self, 1979
Oil on panel, 36 x 49¼
Courtesy of Dan Logan

Arnie Klein, 1980
Oil on panel, 46 x 37
Courtesy of Arnold William Klein, M.D.

David Johns, 1980
Pastel with painted background, 39 x 26
Collection of David G. Johns "Buck"

Franc, 1980
Oil on panel, 27 x 96
Courtesy of Franc Caggiano and Dan Logan

Sam Storm as Napoleon, 1982
Oil on panel, 87½ x 48
Courtesy of Mr. and Mrs. Samuel A. Storm

The Wilders, 1982
Oil on panel, 42½ x 70
Courtesy of Mr. and Mrs. Billy Wilder

California Male, 1983
Oil on canvas, 74 x 50
Courtesy of the Artist

Kenny and Nanci, 1983
Oil on panel, 47⅝ x 45½
Courtesy of Kenneth and Nanci Powell

Selma Holo, 1983
Drawing on toned board, 25 × 40½
Courtesy of Selma Holo

Ariel, 1984
Oil on panel, 53 x 48
Courtesy of Ariel Kelsey Dill

Joan Quinn, 1984
Drawing on toned board, 32 x 40
Collection of Joan and Jack Quinn, Beverly Hills

Marcia Weisman, 1984
Drawing on toned board, 32 x 38
Collection of Marcia S. Weisman, Beverly Hills

Michelle Isenberg, 1984
Drawing on toned board, 32 x 36
Collection of John Moshay, Jr.

Ed Ruscha, 1985
Oil on panel, 59½ x 39½
Courtesy of the Artist

The Gurewitz's, 1985
Drawing on toned board, 40 x 56½
Courtesy of Lorrie and Richard Gurewitz

Pat Maslon, 1985
Drawing with painted background, 35½ x 52½
Courtesy of Patricia J. Maslon

The Jackson Kids, 1986
Oil on panel, 81 x 68
Courtesy of Douglas and Sandi Jackson

Nancy Kattler, 1986
Drawing on toned board, 32¼ x 40¼
Courtesy of Nancy and Bernie Kattler

The Dorens, 1987
Drawing with painted background, 40 x 89
Courtesy of Joan and Jerry Doren

Gary Briskman, 1987
Oil on panel, 90 x 48
Courtesy of Linda and Gary Briskman

My Mother, 1987
Oil on panel, 48½ x 38½
Courtesy of the Artist

The Nortons, 1987
Oil pastel and drawing on painted background,
45 x 77, Courtesy of Eileen and Peter Norton

2 Sisters, 1987
Drawing on painted background, 48¼ x 70⅛
Courtesy of Judy and Edouard Brush

Wena, 1987
Drawing on painted background, diminutive scale,
16 x 25, Courtesy of David and Wena Dows

A Woman at Narita, 1987
Oil on panel, 44⁹/₁₆ x 47⅝
Courtesy of the Artist

Adele at 83, 1988
Drawing with painted background, 39⅜ x 48
Courtesy of the Artist

Singh, 1988
Oil on panel, 56½ x 48
Courtesy of the Artist

Woman in a Chartreuse Sari, 1988
Oil on panel, 66 x 32
Courtesy of the Artist

Gary Briskman, 1987. Oil on panel, 90 x 48

Modern Day Adam and Eve, 1982. Oil on panel, 31½ x 57, (not included in exhibition)

Joan Quinn, 1984. Drawing on toned board 32 x 40

Harrison Moss, 1986. Oil on panel, 55½ x 27
(not included in exhibition)

A Psychiatrist 1981, 1981. Oil on panel, 49 x 53, (not included in exhibition)

A Psychiatrist, Five Years Later 1986, 1986.
Drawing on toned board, 32¼ x 40½, (not included in exhibition)

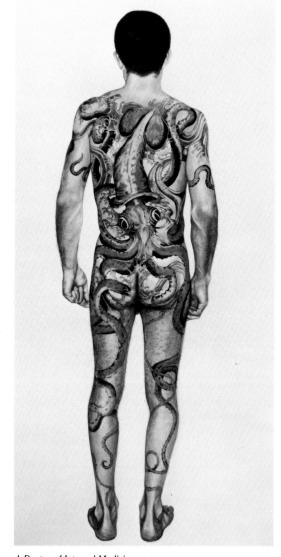

Two of Their Three Bears, 1985. Oil on panel, 74 x 48,
Collection of the Art Museum at FIU, Miami (not included in exhibition)

A Doctor of Internal Medicine, 1980. Oil on panel, 73 x 36,
Collection of the San Antonio Museum, Texas (not included in exhibition)

Sam Storm as Napoleon, 1982. Oil on panel, 87½ x 48

Ed Ruscha, 1985. Oil on panel, 59½ x 39½

Singh, 1988. Oil on panel, 56½ x 48

Woman in a Chartreuse Sari, 1988. Oil on panel, 66 x 32

Sylvia Shap

Born: Toledo, Ohio, 1948
Resides: Los Angeles, California

One Person Exhibitions

1988 *Some Members of My Family,* Los Angeles Municipal Art Gallery, California.

1985 *Sylvia Shap: A Retrospective View,* Simard/Halm Gallery, Los Angeles.

1980 *Sylvia Shap,* Brand Library Art Gallery, Glendale, California.

Selected Group Exhibitions

1988 *Established Artists,* Valerie Miller Fine Art, Palm Desert, California.

Hollywood: Portraits of Stars, Otis Art Institute of Parsons School of Design, Los Angeles.

1987 *Contemporary Southern California Art,* Museum of Fine Arts, Taipei, Taiwan and Los Angeles Municipal Art Gallery.

American Art Today: The Portrait, Art Museum, Florida International University, Miami.

1986 *Looking In — Looking Out: Contemporary Portraits by Women Artists,* Montgomery Gallery, Pomona College, California.

1985 *Off the Street,* Cultural Affairs Department, City of Los Angeles.

1984 *About Face,* Art Museum of South Texas, Corpus Christi; also Art Gallery, Texas Tech University, Lubbock and Nave Museum, Victoria, Texas.

1983 *Facings,* Downey Museum of Art, Downey, California.

1982 *Southern California Realism,* Laguna Museum of Art, Laguna Beach, California.

1981 *Portraits in Miniature,* Fisher Gallery, University of Southern California, Los Angeles.

1980 *Eccentricities: Contemporary Photography,* California Institute of the Arts, Valencia, California; Jurors Joyce Neimanas, Associate Professor, University of Chicago and Van Deren Coke, San Francisco Museum of Modern Art.

1979 *Portraits 79,* Los Angeles Municipal Art Gallery, California.

1978 *First Biennial Show,* Los Angeles Municipal Art Gallery, California.

1976 *L.A. 8 Painting and Sculpture,* Los Angeles County Museum of Art.

1975 *All California Show,* Laguna Museum of Art, Laguna Beach, California.

1974 *California — Hawaii Regional Exhibition,* Fine Arts Gallery, San Diego Museum of Art, California.

Bibliography

Catalogues

Los Angeles Municipal Art Gallery, Cultural Affairs Department, City of Los Angeles, California: *Sylvia Shap: Some Members of My Family.* 1988. Marie de Alcuaz, Curator; Essay by Jim Edwards, Curator, San Antonio Museum of Art.

Museum of Fine Arts. Taipei, Taiwan. Los Angeles Municipal Art Gallery. California. *Contemporary Southern California Art.* 1987 Essay by Marie de Alcuaz, Curator, Los Angeles Municipal Art Gallery.

The Art Museum at Florida International University. Miami, Florida. *American Art Today: The Portrait.* 1987. Essay by Dr. William Betsch, Department of Art and Art History, University of Miami.

Cultural Affairs Department, City of Los Angeles, *Off the Street.* 1985.

Art Museum of Southern Texas. Corpus Christi. *About Face.* 1984. Essay by Jim Edwards, Curator.

Los Angeles County Museum of Art. *L.A. 8: Painting and Sculpture 76.* 1976. Essay by Maurice Tuchman, Senior Curator.

Selected Reviews

Kohen, Helen L. "FIU Exhibition Comes Face to Face with the Portrait," *The Miami Herald,* May 1987.

Ahlander, Leslie J. "Portrait Exhibition Puts FIU's Best Face Forward," *The Miami News,* May 1987.

Firlotte, Gregory. "The Image Makers: Portraits of People in High Places by Sylvia Shap," *Designers West Magazine,* January 1987.

Clothier, Peter. "Exhibition Review," *Art in America,* January 1986.

McCloud, Mac. "Surveying Portraiture," *Artweek,* June 1983.

McDevitt, Lorelei. "Mirror, Mirror on the Wall," *Designers West Magazine,* February 1982.

Muchnic, Suzanne. "Mini-Portraits at USC Art Gallery," *Los Angeles Times,* November 1981

—————— . "Recap of Art Events," *Los Angeles Times,* December 1981.

Wilson, William. "The Portrait: New Life for an Old Form," *Los Angeles Times,* April 1979.

Clothier, Peter. "Looking at Others," *Artweek,* May 1979.

Kogan, Victoria. "How We Really Look," *Artweek,* November 1979.

Muchnic, Suzanne. "Many Called, Few Chosen for Barnsdall," *Los Angeles Times,* May 1978.

Leopold, Michael. "Curator of Contemporary Art Presents 'Surprise' Exhibits," *Society West Magazine,* June 1976.

Marmer, Nancy. "1976: The Dark Underside," *Artforum,* Summer 1976

Professional Listings

1989 *California Artists Calendar,* California International Arts Foundation, Los Angeles

1988 *California Art Review (Second Edition),* American References, Chicago.

Film

1984 *News Focus, Sylvia Shap,* American Broadcasting Company, Corpus Christi, Texas.

1980 *Time Zero,* Promotional Film by Polaroid Land Corporation.

Teaching Appointments

1986 Instructor, Yeshiva University, Los Angeles.

1983 Department of Art, California State University, Fullerton.

Lectures

1987 Museum of Fine Arts, Taipei, Taiwan

1986 - 83 Extension Division, University of California, Los Angeles

1983 California State University, Los Angeles

1980 California State University, Dominguez Hills

Orange Coast College, Costa Mesa, California

1979 Mills House Museum, Garden Grove, California

Los Angeles Municipal Art Gallery, California

Public and Corporate Collections

The Art Museum of South Texas, Corpus Christi
Atlantic Richfield Company, Anchorage, Alaska
Downey Museum of Art, Downey, California
Fisher Gallery, University of Southern California, Los Angeles
The Art Museum at Florida International University, Miami
Music Center, Los Angeles, California
San Antonio Museum of Art, San Antonio, Texas
Victoria Regional Museum, Victoria, Texas

Selected Private Collections

Laddie John Dill, Venice, California
Jesse Dukeminier, Los Angeles
Craig Ellwood, Los Angeles
Susie and Ted Field, Bel Air, CA
Nadja and Stan Frank, La Jolla, CA
Tully Friedman, Los Angeles
Irene and Bob Fritsky, Yardley, PA
Victoria Principal and
  Harry Glassman, M.D., Beverly Hills, CA
Roberta and Robert Greenfield, Brentwood, CA
Sterling Holloway, Laguna Beach, California
Bill Hulse and Corky Korkowski, Humboldt, CA
Sue and Bruce Konheim, Buckeye Construction, Los Angeles
Carol and Frank Lalli, New York
Mrs. Burt Lancaster, Rome, Italy
Ted and Lolly Levy, Los Angeles
A. and K. Lurie, Bel Air, CA
Henry Mancini, Los Angeles
Sandra Moss, Bel Air, CA
Suzanne Muchnic, Los Angeles
Leonard Pennario, Los Angeles
Laurie and Sandi Ratner, La Jolla, CA
Jackie and Manny Silverman, Art Services, Inc., Los Angeles
Maurice Tuchman, Los Angeles
Betty and Ralph Wallerstein, M.D., San Francisco

Franc, 1980. Oil on panel, 27 x 96